THE EARTH EXPERIMENT

A Handbook on Climate Change for the World's Young Keepers

Hwee Goh

Illustrated by **David Liew**

Marshall Cavendish
Children

Published by Marshall Cavendish Children
An imprint of Marshall Cavendish International

A member of the
Times Publishing Group

Other Marshall Cavendish Offices:
Marshall Cavendish Corporation, 800 Westchester Ave, Suite N-641, Rye
Brook, NY 10573, USA • Marshall Cavendish International (Thailand) Co Ltd,
253 Asoke, 16th Flr, Sukhumvit 21 Road, Klongtoey Nua, Wattana, Bangkok
10110, Thailand • Marshall Cavendish (Malaysia) Sdn Bhd, Times Subang,
Lot 46, Subang Hi-Tech Industrial Park, Batu Tiga, 40000 Shah Alam,
Selangor Darul Ehsan, Malaysia

Marshall Cavendish is a registered trademark of Times Publishing Limited

National Library Board, Singapore Cataloguing-in-Publication Data

Name(s): Goh, Hwee. | Liew, David, illustrator.
Title: The experiment : a handbook on climate change for the world's
young keepers / Hwee Goh ; illustrated by David Liew.
Other title(s): Handbook on climate change for the world's young keepers. |
Change makers (Marshall Cavendish Children)
Description: Singapore : Marshall Cavendish Children, [2021]
Identifier(s): OCN 1244773710 | ISBN 978-981-4928-22-9
Subject(s): LCSH: Climatic changes--Juvenile literature. | Global warming--
Juvenile literature. | Nature--effect of human beings on--Juvenile literature.
Classification: DDC   363.73874--dc23

Printed in Singapore

CONTENTS

AN ANCIENT POWER

The world is mostly powered by fossil fuels — these come from living things that have died and decomposed over a long time. The three main fossil fuels are coal, petroleum and natural gas, but the reality is that these will run out.

We Are Recyclables

Plants and animals are made mostly from hydrogen and carbon. When they die, their bodies decompose to become **fossils** that store this "hydrocarbon" energy. Millions of years later, these fossils deep in the ground can be burned to produce new energy. This is how the ancient living world has been a source of **fuel** for our modern one.

What's That?
Fossils are the preserved remains of ancient plants and animals. **Fuel** is any material that is burned to produce heat and power.

Plant and Plankton Power

Scientists say it is a myth that dinosaur remains are part of these fossil fuels, but the coal we burn today does date back to the time dinosaurs roamed **Earth**.

What's That?
When used as a proper noun to refer to our planet, the word "**Earth**" is capitalised.

- **Coal**: Plants decay and turn into peat, a natural layer of moss, which transforms into coal with heat, pressure and time. This was about 300 million years ago, and the reason why it is called the Carboniferous (coal-laden) period.

- **Petroleum**: Small organisms called plankton die and sink to the bottom of ancient seas. The substance is buried and chemically transformed over millions of years. Under pressure and heat, this becomes a hydrocarbon substance we call crude oil, which is refined to become petroleum.

- **Natural gas**: Under even hotter temperatures, these hydrocarbons become natural gas. It also lies in pockets of gas deep in the ground.

I don't get it... Why aren't these dinosaur remains burning?

They'll need to wait a looooong time before those turn into fuel...

Hope they're not hungry.

Takeout hasn't been invented yet, has it?

A Black Rock and a Hard Place

Archaeologists believe that 4,000 years ago, a person in Northern China came across an odd piece of black rock and discovered it could burn. In a time before electricity and gas, this must have been a groundbreaking discovery. By the Han dynasty in the 3rd century BC, these 'stones' were used for fuel and extracting iron ore from the ground.

> ### Did You Know?
> The use of coal worldwide peaks in the early 2000s, driven mainly by the growth of China's economy.

Coal for the Cold

When the Romans ruled the British isles (or Britannia) from the 1st to 4th centuries, it was a time that lumps of "sea coal" could be readily found on beaches. The Romans are credited for inventing central heating, using an external furnace to draw in the heat to warm the floors and walls. They were also said to have loved coal so much for their hot baths, they brought it back to Rome. British coal can still be found in Roman ruins in Italy today.

> **Did You Know?**
> The (over) use of coal only picks up steam during the *Industrial Revolution in Britain.

*See Change Makers: Railroads to Superhighways

Like Oil and Water

The Chinese were known to be drilling into the earth for brine to make salt, discovering natural gas along the way. By the 1st century, they were using iron drills within hollow bamboo pipes to dig downwards. Like most of the other ancients around the world at that time, they were not interested as much in the 石油 (shí yóu), literally stone oil, or crude oil seeping out of the ground. This sticky black mixture was mainly used for medicine, waterproofing and on Egyptian mummies.

Try selling it to the Egyptians. Honestly, I don't know who will find any value in that stuff...

The Black Gold Rush

In 1859, American Edwin Drake famously strikes 'gold' in Titusville, Pennsylvania, hitting a massive oil well 21 m (70 ft) underground. This ignited the black gold rush, much like the rush for gold in California a decade earlier. People started arriving in wagons to tap into this "rock oil" that was found to be an excellent source of kerosene, used for lighting in homes.

Did You Know?
Drake used a similar drilling idea as the Chinese. He drilled inside a hollow iron pipe, so the site would not collapse and fill with water.

Did You Know?
Fossil fuel is now used to produce 80 per cent of the world's electricity. It is also used in many products such as plastics.

I LIVE IN A GREENHOUSE

When fossil fuels burn, carbon is released into the air in the form of carbon dioxide, or CO_2. CO_2 in the atmosphere helps to retain heat from the sun to keep the earth warm, but too much of it has caused a gradual warming of the earth's temperature.

Did You Know?
Weather refers to short term changes in temperature, wind and rain while climate refers to changes over a longer period.

Did You Know?
Climate change is the effect due to global warming, defined as the increase in Earth's temperature since the 1880s (the time of the Industrial Revolution).

It didn't use to be THIS hot...

I wonder if the Ice Age was followed by the Melted Ice Age...

A Question of Simple Physics

When light rays from the sun hit Earth's surface and escape back into the air, why doesn't the planet keep cooling down? It is a logical question that French mathematician Joseph Fourier asks in the 1820s. His instincts tell him there must be a layer in the atmosphere that retains Earth's heat. Without the right physics tools in his time, Fourier's best guess was that it is like a glass box which traps the warm air inside. This notion leads to the concept of "the greenhouse effect".

Did You Know?

The sun's rays are not actually trapped under, but absorbed into the atmosphere, retaining the heat. Carbon dioxide and other 'greenhouse gases' form this layer of insulation.

Did You Know?

Scientists estimate that without greenhouse gases, Earth's temperature would be -18°C.

It's Just Gas

Four decades later, Irish scientist John Tyndall works
in his lab and discovers that gas from coal (which is
a mixture of CO_2, methane and some hydrocarbons)
is especially effective in absorbing heat or energy.
He finds out that CO_2 works like a 'sponge' in absorbing
different rays of sunlight. These gases, together with
water vapour, block the heat from leaving the planet.

What's Your Beef?

The next culprit after CO_2 in greenhouse gas **emission** is methane (CH_4). It comes out on both ends of plant-eating animals like the cow. *Burp!* The cattle industry, which produces milk and beef, is responsible for a fairly large portion of these human-related emissions (because cattle is farmed for human use). One idea has been to use vaccines or another type of plant-food to reduce the amount of gas produced in the cow's gut during digestion.

What's That?
Emission
(to emit) is the release of gas.

Did You Know?
There is much less methane in the atmosphere (compared to CO_2), but it is about 30 times more potent in retaining heat.

Did You Know?
When food is wasted, it not only produces methane when it rots, all the energy used to produce it is also wasted.

Eunice Newton-Foote

I wonder if she would have been discovered earlier if she didn't use her married name?

Well, she DOES have a famous scientific namesake!

You mean her actual name was ISAAC???

Girl Power

Recently, records have surfaced the identity of an American woman scientist Eunice Foote, who experimented with greenhouse gases a few years before Tyndall. She fills glass jars with water vapour, "carbonic gas" (the term for CO_2 then) and air — and compares how much they heat up in the sun. She finds the one with carbonic gas hottest, and it also takes the longest to cool down.

Did You Know?

Foote's maiden name was Newton, and her experiment was discovered in the mid-2010s when another female scientist set out to find women in the history of climate science.

Did You Know?

These discoveries about the potential effects of CO_2 in the 1800s were said to have been received with more curiosity than concern.

15

Ice Age Postponed

At the turn of the 20th century, Swedish scientist **Svante Arrhenius** is looking at how to prevent Earth from falling into another ice age. There have been five ice ages in history which occurred naturally over a long time, due to changes in Earth's orbit around the sun. Arrhenius makes tens of thousands of calculations and comes up with the first climate model which predicts that CO_2 causes global warming. He proves mathematically that:

- If the level of CO_2 in the atmosphere is halved, Earth's surface temperature would fall.

- The reverse is also true — a doubling of CO_2 would raise temperatures, delaying an ice age season.

Who's That?

Svante Arrhenius is the 1903 Nobel Prize winner for Chemistry, and known as the father of climate science. Swedish teenage climate activist Greta Thunberg (page 60) is related to him through her father Svante Thunberg.

Did You Know?

There was a Little Ice Age as recent as the 14th to 19th centuries, with a global dip in temperature and expanding ice caps. Scientists believe that volcanic eruptions created a layer of ash in Earth's upper atmosphere, which deflected sun rays back into space.

Wow, he was already seeing trouble way back then...

I guess nobody listened to him.

But Greta sure did...

HOW DARE YOU!

Svante Arrhenius

Greta Thunberg

MY CARBON FOOTPRINT

By all accounts, humans have made a definite impact on Earth. The use of fossil fuels and the resulting CO_2 emissions can no longer be dismissed. We are producing far more CO_2 than Earth can handle.

Earth's Breathing Cycle

Just how much CO_2 is there left in the atmosphere after nature has absorbed it? This was the question geochemist Charles Keeling sought to answer in the 1950s, and the Keeling Curve was born. It shows global CO_2 levels going up and down in a jagged manner, depending on the season. However, the whole Keeling Curve continues to move upwards every year.

Did You Know?

Scientists today still continue to collect CO_2 readings at the Mauna Loa Observatory in Hawaii, where Keeling worked until his death in 2005.

The Invisible Pollutant

Keeling was the first to confirm the link between burning fossil fuels and the release of CO_2 into the atmosphere. His numbers also proved that about half of this CO_2 does not get absorbed by forests and oceans, but accumulates as greenhouse gas. Scientists are able to identify CO_2 coming from fossil fuels by the lack of carbon-14, a type of carbon that is long decayed from fossils.

Not a Toe-Print

In 1992, Canadian William Rees invents the "ecological footprint" to measure our impact on the environment. This evolves to become the term "carbon footprint", which measures the total emission of CO_2 per year. Every person, company or country is able to calculate this, and it should not just include electricity used, but everything from the farming of the meat we eat, to the whole process of the petrol used in the car we drive or ride in.

Did You Know?
The unit of measurement for carbon footprint is CO_2e (carbon dioxide equivalent). It represents the total impact of all greenhouse gases used. Besides methane, there are also nitrous oxide and refrigerant gases used in all cooling systems.

Just as well you're not around anymore. Your footprint would be HUGE in every sense of the word...

Well, he's still sort of around — inside fossil fuels!

Argh! That joke is as old as the fossils!

The 400 ppm Milestone

On 9 May 2013, the Mauna Loa Observatory recorded a CO_2 reading of 400 ppm, a number scientists were nervously waiting for. It was the first time in 55 years of measurements that this number had been reached. The last time it was believed to be this high was during the Pliocene, an **epoch** 3 million years ago.

What's That?

An **epoch** defines the age of Earth based on the geology, or the layers of rock in the earth at that time. We are currently in the Holocene, an epoch that began about 12,000 years ago.

Did You Know?

Scientists are able to estimate CO_2 levels from up to 800,000 years ago, by measuring CO_2 directly from bubbles trapped in ancient ice in the Antarctic.

Eh? Weren't they looking for gas trapped in the ice?

Yes, but not THIS kind of gas!

Smells like somebody in the Palaeolithic period had onions for dinner!

Fun fact: Carbon dioxide is colourless and odourless.

Editor's note: Flatulence is colourless too, but we had to allow this one to be coloured.

A Year in the Life of Carbon Dioxide

In 2014, the National Aeronautics and Space Administration (NASA) launches the Orbiting Carbon Observatory-2 (OCO-2) into space. By measuring sunlight as it passes through the atmosphere and reflects back up — it calculates how much CO_2 is in the air. About 100,000 such measurements are taken a day from 15 orbits around Earth. The amount of CO_2 is measured in parts per million (ppm) or how many parts of CO_2 there are in a million parts of air.

Did You Know?

NASA provides measurements of CO_2 in our atmosphere.

Scan to check it out!

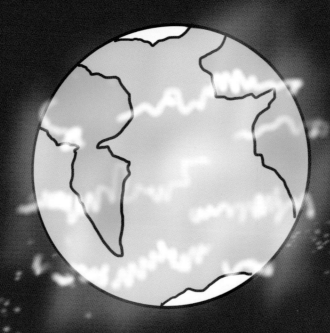

Polar Lessons from the Pliocene

It is not known what caused the greenhouse effect during the Pliocene, except that it was natural and not man-made. However, the time it takes for Earth to reach 400 ppm now is much faster, toward a climate future nobody can predict.

During the Pliocene:

- The planet was about 2°C to 3°C warmer.
- Sea levels were at least 9 m (30 ft) higher than now — a level that would drown out major cities in this world.
- A small change in global temperature was amplified in the polar regions. The icy cold and dry Canadian High Arctic, normally -18°C, was much warmer. A fossil find in 2013 confirmed that a large camel species lived in a forested region there.

Living in the Anthropocene

In February 2000, Nobel laureate Paul Crutzen argues that humans are now the driving force behind Earth, using "anthropo-" to mean humans and "-cene" to refer to this new epoch we now live in. It is a term that has caught on in the news and culture, reflecting the urgency of human impact on the climate. What will geologists in the far future find in our layers of rock — CO_2, plastics, mobile phones and building debris?

Did You Know?
Geologists are not yet agreed on whether we are in the Anthropocene, but those who do are divided over whether it started from the Industrial Revolution in the 1800s, or after the 1945 atomic bomb (when radioactive soil samples were found globally).

THE EARTH EXPERIMENT

The last decade was the hottest on record, and 2020 was the hottest year ever. The question now is whether global warming will keep trending upward, causing hottest to become even hotter.

Did You Know?

The UN Secretary-General António Guterres has called on people to change the game on the climate, before the climate changes our lives forever.

"Making peace with nature is the defining task of the 21st century. It must be the top priority for everyone, everywhere."

What's That?

To **change the game** is to do something to change the direction for the better.

A Global Chain Reaction

Since the late 19th century, the global temperature has gone up about 1°C. Such a seemingly small number has had devastating effects on everything — the weather, the oceans and all creatures big and small. The excessive burning of fossil fuels, releasing CO_2 which causes global warming, has made this a giant "**geoengineering**" experiment for Earth.

> **What's That?**
> **Geoengineering** is to make large scale changes to how the planet works, to slow down or reverse the effects of climate change.

Too HOT to Be Cool

The impact of higher temperatures is no longer a concept in a far-flung future. Changes due to a warming Earth is happening right here, right now.

- Ice melts: Glaciers and ice sheets are melting, especially at the earth's poles. Animals that live in icy regions are losing their habitat, or homes.

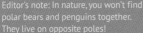

Editor's note: In nature, you won't find polar bears and penguins together. They live on opposite poles!

- Sea levels rise: Low-lying islands and countries may lose their land, and animals and plants living near shorelines may die out.

- Migration: When it is too warm, animals seek cooler regions to survive. Some do not make it.

- Under the sea: Excess CO_2 is absorbed by the oceans, making the water more acidic. This makes it harder for some corals and organisms to survive.

A Climate Catastrophe

Warmer temperatures collide with cooler air, creating weather disasters and distress over the last two decades.

- Greater evaporation: Higher temperatures cause plants and soil to lose water, making the climate in drier regions even warmer.

- Extreme heat waves: These are periods of abnormally hot weather, lasting days to weeks. Intense heat waves have caused droughts and uncontrolled wildfires.

- Flooding: Warm air expands, forcing winds to spiral upward. As the winds cool, water vapour condenses and falls as rain. Together with rising sea levels, heavy rains cause floods, disrupting lives.

- Hurricanes: Warmer temperatures and sea surfaces are causing more superstorms coming from the oceans. Scientists are also studying trends in severe snow and thunderstorms.

SCIENCE OF THE SEAS

Humans have a direct hand in the CO_2 they produce, driving up temperatures and melting the world's ice sheets into the sea. What we have underestimated is the power of the massive ocean in tempering the effects of global warming. Even so, it cannot cope anymore. Every **molecule** of CO_2 that we do not put into the air now is important to our future.

What's That?

CO_2 is a **molecule** made up of one carbon atom and two oxygen atoms. When fossil fuels (hydrocarbons) are burnt, carbon combines with oxygen to form CO_2.

MOTHER EARTH   NEPTUNE

A Giant Buffer

Even in the late 19th century, scientists already suspected that CO_2 in the atmosphere could cause global warming. What they could not figure out was why it was not as hot as they had calculated. Where was the missing heat? As it turns out, our oceans have been hard at work absorbing most of this excess heat caused by greenhouse gases.

The Ocean Pays the Price

Fish and other sea creatures breathe oxygen and give off CO_2. Ocean plants take in CO_2 and give off oxygen. As it is, our vast ocean is already helping to suck up about a quarter of the CO_2 from fossil fuels. The problem is, besides causing higher temperatures, the CO_2 also makes the sea water more acidic.

(NIGHTMARE) VISION OF THE *FUTURE?

Welcome to
EVEREST
BASE CAMP

ELEVATION:
15 METRES ABOVE SEA LEVEL

Yeti
Surf
Rentals

✳ WHICH MAY BE NEARER THAN WE THINK...

Stem the Tide

The entire top slice of the ocean from the surface to 2 km (6,500 ft) below has been the warmest ever. On average, sea temperatures go up by a tenth of a degree every year, but this increase nudges sea levels up. Warmer water expands and takes up more space, but also holds less oxygen and could hurt marine life.

Did You Know?
Sea levels have swelled over 20 cm (8 in) since 1880, mostly in the last few decades. The planet's oceans have been the hottest on record, through the 2010s.

Just the Tip of the Iceberg

Huge sheets of ice on earth are like protective white spots that help to reflect excess heat from the sun back into space. As this ice melts, the dark ocean absorbs more heat, making the overall temperature even higher.

- Glaciers are formed on land, and most of the earth's glacial ice is on the Antarctic in the south. When the ice melts, the water runs off into the ocean.

- The Greenland ice cap on the Arctic in the north is disappearing fast. If it all melted, global sea levels could rise by 7 m (20 ft).

- Sea ice is like an ice cube in a glass of water and when melted, does not change the water level. However, when sea ice melts, arctic wildlife like walruses and polar bears lose their homes and hunting grounds.

The Power of Frozen

Until it was discovered in the 1820s, nobody had set eyes on the icy continent of Antarctica. Nobody lives there but scientists work there in the summer, and tourists visit. The massive landform of East Antarctica hovers around -55°C, a number way below freezing that has been able to withstand global warming. Recently though, scientists have reported some ice loss.

Did You Know?

Several countries have laid claim to parts of it, but the 1959 Antarctic Treaty, signed by 50 plus nations, aims to preserve the territory for peace and science.

Did You Know?

Although the East Antarctic core plateau is extremely cold and sturdy, the warming ocean waters on its edges have caused ice shelves to collapse into the sea. The West Antarctic ice sheet is more unstable and a threat to sea levels.

Tiny but Mighty

Argo is an international programme that has a fleet of more than 4,000 robotic sensors that collect information from the oceans. Since most of the excess heat from greenhouse gases goes into the ocean, this gives a better measure of global warming than from the air. Argo floats work in tandem with Jason satellites which collect Earth's data from space. In Greek mythology, Jason sailed on his ship, Argo, in search of the golden fleece.

WE ARE SINKING!

Could you imagine living in a walled city below sea level? Or losing your home completely when it gets washed away by the ocean? Global sea levels have risen as much as 20 cm (8 in) in the last century. If CO_2 emissions continue to go up, the sea could rise much more by 2100.

Ground Zero of Climate Change

Based on history, global warming is likely to be **amplified** at the extremes of the earth. The Arctic is warming twice as fast as the rest of the planet. The northernmost US town of Barrow, Alaska is feeling the very effects of it. The thick layer of ice, or permafrost, it stands on is thawing and causing roads and buildings to buckle. Where sea ice used to protect the coastline from strong winds and storms, the loss of this ice has brought flooding.

Did You Know?

In 2008, a wildfire broke out north of Brooke Range (a mountain range in the Arctic) where the locals did not even have the vocabulary for "forest fire".

What's That?

To **amplify** is to make the effects greater. Scientists say that based on history and geology, the situation in Alaska is an "early warning system" for the rest of the world.

Sponge Cities

Most of China's largest cities are affected by flooding, especially the ones by the coast. In 2014, it started the Sponge City Concept. The idea is that a city plans its tunnels, roads and ponds to soak up as much extra water as possible during seasonal storms. This water is 'stored' to prevent flooding and can be re-used during times of drought. In view of global warming and flooding, China's plan is to equip another 600 cities this decade.

Did You Know?

Shanghai is most in danger of "sinking" and so are 10 other Asian cities. A study in 2020 listed Tokyo, Bangkok, Jakarta and Ho Chi Minh city, together with Dubai and New York City, among the world's top 15 cities most at risk from rising sea levels.

Did You Know?

Another Sponge City, Singapore also uses (free) storm water. Its Rain Vortex at Jewel Changi Airport collects rainwater through a huge transparent funnel into an indoor garden below. The water is re-used within the building.

Sponge City?

No, City Sponge.

Hey, is that a PINEAPPLE over there?

Fight or Flight

In South East Asia, cities like Manila and Jakarta are working on long-term plans to move their capital cities to higher ground. Sitting at barely 5 m (16.5 ft) above sea level, Singapore is putting up a $100 billion plan over the next 100 years to stay put. It plans to:

- Strengthen 80 per cent of the country's shoreline.
- Use natural barriers like mangroves and sea grasses against flooding.
- Impose a carbon tax on businesses that burn fossil fuels, and consumers who use electricity.

> **Did You Know?**
> Kiribati, a group of islands on the Pacific Ocean, has bought one of the Fiji Islands 2,000 km (1,243 mi) away, in case its own lands disappear from rising sea levels. Maldives, however, is building a new artificial island called Hulhumalé or "City of Hope".

LEGENDARY* DUTCH
ANTI-FLOOD MEASURES

HANS BRINKER

AKA "THE LITTLE DUTCH BOY"

✳ AND MOST LIKELY TOTALLY FICTIONAL

That Sinking Feeling

In late January 1953, the sea off the coast of the Netherlands rose so high, it broke the dykes, or storm walls, in the southwest. The villagers of Oude-Tonge saw their streets and houses collapse before their eyes. Since then, the government has spent billions to save the low-lying country from flooding ever again. Even so, as the world looks to the Dutch for lessons on rising sea levels, the Dutch are also questioning if their defences are good enough.

Did You Know?
A third of the Netherlands lies below sea level.

Did You Know?
Hans Brinker or the Silver Skates, is an 1865 novel written by American author Mary Mapes Dodge. There is a tale in it that has become legend — a Dutch boy saves his village from flooding, by sticking his finger into a leaking dyke.

Superstorm Sandy

The National Geographic called it "a raging freak of nature". In late October 2012, a tropical cyclone forms over the Caribbean sea, off the coast of Nicaragua. Over nine days, it reacts with winds and higher, warmer seas along the way and becomes a superstorm. It goes on to wreak havoc through the Caribbean and major cities on the east coast of the US.

Did You Know?
Tropical cyclones form over warm ocean waters, mixing with cooler air to become storms. They are called "hurricanes" over the North Atlantic and Northeast Pacific, but "typhoons" over the Northwest Pacific Ocean.

Did You Know?
Although scientists cannot confirm that climate change causes more hurricanes, warmer seas and higher sea levels can make them stronger and more destructive.

43

A PLASTIC PLANET

Plastics have been getting a lot of attention
for how much waste they generate, but not
for their role in global warming and climate change.
They are very much part of the carbon cycle,
from the fossil fuels extracted to make them,
to the CO_2 released to produce, transport
and dispose of them.

A Miracle Invention

In the mid 19th century, the popular game of billiards is threatened by a shrinking supply of ivory balls, made from elephant tusks. A company in New York puts up a prize of $10,000 for anyone who is able to find a substitute. John Wesley Hyatt shapes the world's first **plastic** by mixing cellulose from cotton, wax from the camphor tree, and alcohol. He doesn't win the prize but he does go on to supply the first 'celluloid' plastic to make day-to-day items.

Did You Know?

In the 1800s, skilled craftsmen had to ensure billiard balls were made from the centre of the elephant tusk so that they would "roll true". The demand for ivory (also for piano keys and trinkets) increases the hunt for Asian elephants.

What's That?

The word **plastic** is from the Greek word *plastikos* which refers to something that can be moulded into any shape.

Did Mr Hyatt get his synthetic elephant ivory from synthetic elephants?

Too bad it didn't stop the poaching.

Did You Know?

George Eastman (of Kodak) used celluloid as the first flexible film for photos and movies, which is why the term is also used to mean movies.

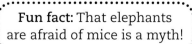

Fun fact: That elephants are afraid of mice is a myth!

Fame and Shame

Before plastics were invented, everything humans built was from nature: wood, metal, stone, tusk and bone. For the first time, many new things could be made with plastic.

- Plastics were touted as the saviour of animals that now did not need to be killed.
- Countless lives are saved by plastics in healthcare, used in medical devices.
- Even clean energy relies on plastics, like wind turbines and solar panels.
- This also means plastic is everywhere, making it the planet's worst environmental problem.

Fossil Fuel Plastics

Leo Baekeland, a Belgian immigrant in New York, is the one who coins the term "plastic". In 1907, he creates synthetic plastic with phenol from coal tar and formaldehyde, distilled from wood alcohol. He calls it Bakelite, the world's first plastic made from fossil fuel. Once heated and formed, it is indestructible and resistant to heat. It is used for electrical insulation, cabinets, countertops and (yes) billiard balls.

Did You Know?
Bakelite also became an essential ingredient for weapons used in World War II.

What's That?
Synthetic materials are made from chemical or artificial substances.

Waste Not, Want Not

By the 1960s, the tide starts to turn against the popularity of plastic when it shows up in the world's oceans.

- Plastic does not break down for hundreds of years and lives on in vast oceans, as well as in micro bits of plastic swallowed by sea creatures. We literally might eat our own trash.

- It releases greenhouse gases from the day it is produced, until it is incinerated (burnt as garbage).

- Interestingly, humans generate even more invisible waste in CO_2 emissions, than trash.

Did You Know?

Scientists argue that plastics and climate are two sides of the same coin, and both urgently need to be addressed.

The Great Pacific Garbage Patch

The poor ocean has been handling the world's trash as well. The gyre, a large system of rotating ocean currents, delivers plastic waste from our waters and holds it together in the north of the Pacific Ocean. This island of floating plastic trash is estimated to be 1.6 million km² (618,000 mi²) which is roughly three times the size of France.

Did You Know?

Some countries still pay to ship their plastic waste to poorer countries where people earn their living sorting it through. What is not recycled usually gets incinerated, further polluting the air. Other countries with abundant land literally bury the problem in landfills, but space is running out.

A Recycling Revolution

Less than 10 per cent of plastics get recycled every year. The game changer is going to be a "zero-waste" plan where plastic never becomes waste.

- Some plastics are already being processed into pellets to be reused for making new plastics.
- Plastics, which are made up of hydrocarbons, can be converted back into fuel.
- "Bioplastics" are made from plants so that they are biodegradable and will break down naturally.

Did You Know?

Reused plastic has been made into new shoes, skateboards and other products. There are roads in Melbourne, Australia, that are paved with material recycled from plastic bags, glass and printer cartridges.

Did You Know?

Sweden has a waste-to-energy (WTE) programme that converts the energy from burning trash, to heat and electricity.

THE BUTTERFLY EFFECT

Global warming and climate change have brought to the fore, the idea that **minute** changes in temperature caused by excessive CO_2, will lead to large unpredictable events like superstorms, flooding and, not least the loss of animals and plants.

What's That?
minute (mai-newt):
Very tiny.

Chaos Theory

The butterfly effect predicts that the flap of a butterfly's wings in one part of the world might cause a tornado in another. It was a concept made popular in weather science by Edward Lorenz in the 1960s. Lorenz's mathematical theory found that a small change in conditions could produce 'chaos', and a large number of different, unpredictable outcomes.

Did You Know?

A 2015 study in England ran a reverse calculation and found that CO_2 emissions and a 2°C increase in global temperature could wipe out some butterfly species.

Did You Know?

Science fiction writer Ray Bradbury's *A Sound of Thunder* (1952) is about a man who travels 65 million years back in time to shoot a dinosaur. He panics at the sight of a tyrannosaur, and steps on and crushes a butterfly under his boot. He returns to a completely changed world.

Sea Butterflies

The ocean's chemistry has changed, becoming more acidic as it absorbs excess CO_2. This dissolves the shells of an important species called pteropods, also known as sea butterflies for the way they flutter and move with wing-like extensions. These **molluscs** are a very important part of the food web, and if they die off, could affect the organisms above them, including humans.

What's That?

There are at least 50,000 known species of **molluscs**, including snails, octopuses, scallops and clams.

Did You Know?

About 250 million years ago, excessive CO_2 from volcanic eruptions caused a similar acidification of the oceans, killing off more than 90 per cent of marine species. This period coincided with the Permian-Triassic extinction (page 56).

We may have lost our shells, but poor old Pteropod has dissolved totally!

White Ocean Skeletons

Corals are highly sensitive to temperature change, and a warming of just 1°C causes them to spit out the colourful algae that live inside them, losing their source of nutrition. This is known as coral bleaching. In recent years, 75 per cent of the world's coral reefs have been under severe heat stress, also causing them to become diseased. Some do not recover.

Heyah! Welcome to the club...

MUSEUM OF NATURAL HISTORY
EXTINCT ANIMALS SECTION

BRAMBLE CAY MELOMYS
EXTINCT

Fun fact: This bird is often used as an example of an extinct animal. What is it?

Simply No More

In the mid 1800s, the mosaic-tailed rat (named for the pattern on its tail) was first spotted by Europeans on an island near Australia's Great Barrier Reef. It was also called the Bramble Cay melomys, after the island, the only place it could be found. With rising sea levels, the low-lying island has shrunk, wiping out the rodent's home. In 2016, the Australian government declared it **extinct**.

Did You Know?

The Bramble Cay melomys is said to be the first mammal to be a casualty of climate change.

What's That?

A species (spee-shees) becomes **extinct** when a type of plant or animal can no longer be found anywhere in the world.

Answer: Dodo

The Sixth Mass Extinction

By studying geology and the layers of rock formation, scientists have been able to conclude that there were five mass extinctions in our past, wiping out an estimated 70 to 95 per cent of all species each time.

Ordovician-Silurian Extinction 440 million years ago	Devonian Extinction 365 million years ago	Permian-Triassic Extinction 250 million years ago
Massive ice sheets made a cold planet impossible to survive in, as sea levels also fell.	Also known as the "age of fish", there were few land animals. Marine creatures died off when oxygen levels in the sea dropped.	The "Great Dying" was caused by a complex of volcanoes across where Siberia is now. Global warming and loss of oxygen made this the worst event recorded.

Earth's sixth mass extinction is said to be happening now, and it is caused by humans. Scientists warn that species are going extinct a hundred times faster than they would in nature, and we could approach mass extinction in the next few centuries.

Triassic-Jurassic Extinction 210 million years ago	Cretaceous-Paleogene Extinction 65 million years ago
Ancient lava flows caused huge amounts of greenhouse gases, global warming and CO_2 acidification of the oceans.	The most recent mass extinction involving land dinosaurs was caused by a major asteroid.

Time Machine

Climate change killed the dinosaurs.

But that was an act of nature...

Whereas man is wiping HIMSELF out.

Heal the World

Many parts of Earth have seen a 1.5°C increase in temperature, which is already affecting every aspect of the planet's health. Scientists are calling for the world to do everything possible to keep CO_2 lower than 450 ppm, so that global warming stays below 2°C. In the Anthropocene, if people, businesses and governments act, every small change could have an amplified, or greater, benefit to the climate.

Did You Know?

Almost 200 countries signed the 2015 Paris Agreement, which pledges to keep global warming well below 2°C and to maintain it at 1.5°C, if possible.

INHERIT THE EARTH

A new generation of Earth's keepers are growing up. They no longer face a simple call to reduce-reuse-recycle, or a **tree-hugging** appeal to "save the polar bears" for our future. They inherit an earth already in a climate emergency, and they are the ones who will pay the price if nothing is done.

What's That?

The term **tree hugger** was first used in 1730, when 360 men and women in India were killed while trying to 'hug' and protect the trees in their village from being chopped down to build a new palace. It is a term now used on people who are overly emotional about protecting the environment.

GO AWAY!

TREE HUGGING POLAR BEAR

Our House Is on Fire

In August 2019, Swedish teenager Greta Thunberg sailed on a solar-powered yacht (reducing her carbon footprint) across the Atlantic to the United Nations Climate Action Summit. Millions all over the world gathered in support of her. In her speech to the world's leaders, she said:

Did You Know?

Thunberg has Asperger's syndrome, which is on the autism spectrum. It has given her a straightforwardness with her words, which she calls her "superpower".

- The climate science has been "crystal clear" for the last 30 years, and yet the politics and solutions for change are nowhere in sight.

- Based on current CO_2 emissions targets to cap global warming at 1.5°C, there is only a 50 per cent chance of success. This is not acceptable to her generation, who will have to deal with the fallout.

Did You Know?

The UNCRC started in 1989 with governments pledging to protect the rights of the child to survival.

Thunberg and 15 other activists (aged 8 to 17) also filed a legal complaint with the United Nations Convention on the Rights of the Child (UNCRC) against the top greenhouse gas-producing countries.

Solar...
sigh

The Math and Science of Climate

The world's scientists are in agreement with this "Earth Experiment" on climate change. The extent of global warming is directly related to how much CO_2 we produce. The only way to stabilise temperatures is to bring CO_2 to "net zero" by 2050.

Zero in on Zero

Net zero, is to be carbon- or climate neutral, which means only as much CO_2 is released as it is absorbed or removed. This means:

- Cutting down on mining and burning of fossil fuels.

- Switching to cleaner energy like solar, wind and even nuclear power.

- Industries with a heavy carbon footprint need to 'offset' their CO_2 emissions by paying for carbon-reduction activities elsewhere, such as planting trees that will absorb CO_2.

Many key European countries, as well as China, Japan and Korea, have set laws to reach net zero carbon emissions, mostly by the year 2050.

Did You Know?

Since the 1990s, there has been a 'carbon market' where companies buy, sell and trade carbon. Even an individual taking a flight, for example, can buy carbon credit to offset the CO_2 produced from the journey.

Who'd think that we'd be pioneers of clean energy!

MOTHER NATURE'S CLIMATE LAB

The solution is an oldie but goodie!

Natural Climate Solutions

What is a giant device that can suck CO_2 out of the air? A tree! Rather than box in nature as a victim of climate change, nature can also be the most powerful solution. It means governments and companies have to incorporate grass and wetlands into their planning, as well as reforest land as much as they can.

Did You Know?

A new technology called carbon capture diverts CO_2 emissions and stores it underground or recycles it through a process that converts it into liquid fuel.

Did You Know?

Natural climate solutions might be able to reduce CO_2 emissions by a third, but the rest will have to rely on new ideas in science and technology.

A Pizza Box of Energy

Scientists at the **Pentagon** are working on a solar panel from space, the size of a pizza box. It is currently attached to an unmanned drone that goes round Earth every 90 minutes. High up there, it is able to use the energy from blue light waves, which usually bounce off the atmosphere (giving the sky its blue colour). On a large scale, solar energy from space could provide us with fossil fuel-free electricity.

Did You Know?
Blue light has a very short wavelength and so produces a higher amount of energy. This is the same reason why it could damage the eyes if exposed to it over a long period of time.

What's That?
The **Pentagon** is named for the five-sided building which houses the US Army, Navy and Airforce.

Sink or Swim

Every tenth of a degree in global warming is worth fighting against. There may be divisions in politics among countries, but the truth is that all will sink or swim in the time of climate change. Climate science leaders have urged countries not to "greenwash" their net zero plans just to look good. Rather, there needs to be a commitment by every Earth citizen to make this change happen.

WE'RE IN THIS TOGETHER!

MY Chemistry NOTES

Dear Reader,

You have been born into a world with climate change. Now that you have read *The Earth Experiment*, how do you think the world should change along with it?

In this section, you could map out the chain reaction of CO_2 emissions on global warming and our oceans. Or you could plan how you will change the game, by reducing your carbon footprint.

Let's do this together!

Love,

[signatures] &

HWEE'S HANDBOOK TOOLKIT

Climate change is one of very few areas that the adults in your life probably have not done better. I certainly haven't. This is your world, and you will take the lead for change. Here, I have mapped out some ideas to send you on your way to greatness!

Science Is True
Whether You Believe It or Not

Astrophysicist Neil deGrasse Tyson said this, and science is indeed our best weapon. If we know the definite science that causes global warming and climate change, we also know the definite science to solve this.

Never Too Late

The issue of climate change may bring about a sense of hopelessness — that we are too late. The strategy now is to (1) cut greenhouse gases by a significant amount in the near future but (2) adapt to changes that have been set in motion, such as rising sea levels. However, a true solution needs a global response.

Good Is the Enemy of Great

Is it good enough if your government or local business is pledging to go net zero? If we are already in a climate emergency, solutions have to make a difference to the future of you, Earth's young keeper. Write letters, share your knowledge and persuade others to act.

These are good, BUT still NOT GOOD ENOUGH!

Be Your Own Butterfly

Build your own circle of impact. If everybody does so, they can create a butterfly effect on climate change. Research ways you can reduce your carbon footprint — make sure to turn off the lights when not in use, cut down on food waste and take public transport.

ACKNOWLEDGEMENTS

Lots of Thank Yous to:

Lydia Leong, my editor, for your firm yet indulgent way with us.

Izzy, my best beta reader.

PUB, Singapore's National Water Agency.

Fellow journalists, commentators and especially the National Geographic and NASA.

Climate scientists since the 19th century, for putting their instincts to the test and laying the groundwork for what we know today.

ABOUT
HWEE AND DAVID

Trained at the Northwestern University Medill School of Journalism, former CNA (Channel NewsAsia) reporter and editor **Hwee Goh** put together this handbook from current 2021 climate change titles and a few hundred sources online. Hwee, who is a media and editorial consultant, is also a veteran on the school circuit. She continues to curate stories on @hweezbooks.

Illustrator **David Liew** and Hwee were in junior college together studying strange but true moments in history. They grew up being warned that climate change is coming. This book is the least they could do for young readers who are now born into it. David taught history, before becoming illustrator to many bestselling book series. David's art often takes on humorous angles appreciated by his fans, young and old. It is with this added layer of art that the Change Makers team hopes to engage young readers on their own journey.